TEMPLE
SAGRADA FAMÍLIA

Text: Jordi Bonet i Armengol

Photographs, design, lay-out and printing, entirely created
by the technical department of
EDITORIAL ESCUDO DE ORO, S.A.

Editorial Escudo de Oro, S.A.

Engraving of the city of Barcelona, at the foot of Montjuïc Castle.

THE HISTORICAL SETTING

The Sagrada Familia is the product of the circumstances stemming from its foundation and the unique drive of Antoni Gaudí, who devoted more than 40 years of his life as an architect to it.

The Catholic faith, which had a strong presence in the origins of Catalonia in the 10th century, again played a leading role in the nation's rebirth –the «Renaixença», or Renaissance– one thousand years later, when workers, farmers and intellectuals, amongst them the country-born priest and poet Jacint Verdaguer, restored their language to its rightful dignity.

The expansion of the city of Barcelona, with the industrial revolution and the impulse of the bourgeoisie, brought into being a powerful capital city where art flourished alongside trade and the economy.

Catalonia once again opened up to the world, generously regaling it with all its finest and most personal achievements.

At a difficult moment for the Universal Church, a Barcelona bookseller, Josep Maria Bocabella, created the Association of Followers of Saint Joseph to give spiritual and material aid to the Holy See, proposing, moreover, to build a monumental church, dedicated to the Holy Family, to be surrounded by gardens, where respectable public leisure activities would be complemented by learning, education and spiritual contemplation.

FOUNDING AND CORNERSTONE

A notarial document «bears witness that the Bishop of Barcelona, Josep Maria Urquinaona i Bidot, cloaked in the sacred ornaments and attended by the Bishop Elect of Vic, Dr Josep Morgades and other members of the clergy, in presence of the Captain General and other dignitaries, of Josep Maria Bocabella and Manuel de Dalmases, representing the Followers of Saint Joseph, of the architect F. P. De Villar, Elias Rogent, Director of the School of Architecture, and a large gathering of the faithful, solemnly proceeded to bless the land, placing the cornerstone of a Monumental Expiatory Church, to the greater glory of the Holy Family. To awaken from their slumbers the lukewarm heart, exalt the Faith, promote Charity, Invoke the Lord to have mercy on this country so that, encouraged by its Catholic roots, it will think, preach and practice the Virtues» (parchment text deposited in the cornerstone on 19 March 1882). The walls of the crypt were about to be built when, due to disagreements with the Followers of Joseph, the architect and author of the project resigned. In around November 1883, a promising new architect, Antoni Gaudí i Cornet was commissioned to carry out the work.

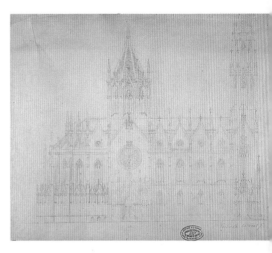

Outline and west front of the church.

The founder, Josep Maria Bocabella.

Gaudí attended the first reading of Verdaguer's poem «Canigó».

Antoni Gaudí I Cornet. ▷

GAUDÍ, ARCHITECT OF THE SAGRADA FAMILIA

Antoni Gaudí, born on 26 June 1852, was baptised in the Church of Sant Pere in Reus, then Catalonia's second city. The future architect's family were coppersmiths who struggled to give the young Gaudí an education. Reus was a dynamic, prosperous provincial city which, in the space of just a few years, produced such other men of great renown as Joan Prim, the general who became president of the Spanish government, and Marià Fortuny, a painter famous throughout Europe in the mid-19th century.

Having obtained his degree in architecture from the Barcelona School of Architecture in 1878, Gaudí soon distinguished himself in his chosen field of activity, receiving commissions from the man who would be his friend and patron, Eusebi Güell i Bacigalupi, as well as from the prestigious architect, Joan Martorell, who involved him in the Sagrada Familia project. He was also friendly with poet Joan Maragall, one of the great sponsors of the enterprise.

4

Aerial view of the Church of the Sagrada Familia.

DESCRIPTION

Antoni Gaudí envisaged the Church of the Sagrada Familia emerging from the urban landscape of Barcelona in dramatic verticality. The church has a basilica groundplan, with a nave, four aisles and a transept with a nave and two aisles. The interior is 90 metres in length and the transept is 60 metres wide. The nave in the centre measures 15 metres and the apse is bordered by 17th century chapels and 2 circular staircases, with an ambulatory around the presbytery. An outer cloister encircles the building, connecting the three entrance façades, or fronts. These are, to the east, that of the Nativity; to the west, that of the Passion, and to the south, that of the Glory. Each of these fronts is crowned by four belltowers symbolising the twelve apostles. There is a sacristy at each corner of the apse wall. The Chapel of the Holy Sacrament and the Baptistery occupy the corners at either side of the Front of the Glory. A 170 metre high dome rises in the centre of the transept representing Jesus Christ, flanked by a further four symbolising the Evangelists. Over the apse is another, dedicated to the Mother of God.

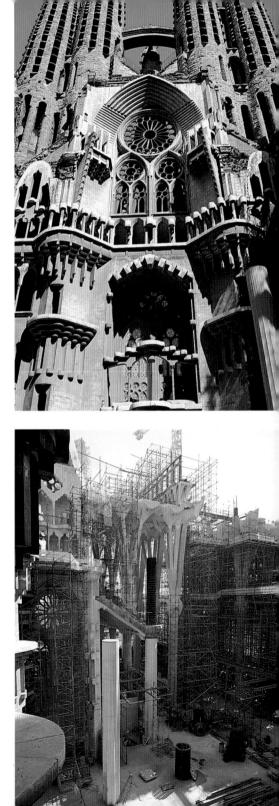

Interior of the east front.

1.- The groundplan

The groundplan takes the shape of a Latin cross, its longest arm almost as long from the transept to the rear of the apse as the Portal of Glory. Gaudí maintained the orientation of the axes as his predecessor had begun the church, though he would rather have placed it diagonally.

The church has a nave and two aisles, the nave 15 metres wide, the aisles 7.5 metres in width, complemented by a further aisle on either side occupying at a greater height the singers' galleries at the front of the crossing, making a total width of 45 metres.

A huge inner space measuring 900 m² with four central columns occupies the centre of the transept, which rises to a height of 60 metres. The entire inner space is encircled by the cloister and the three portals, with sacristies on either side of the apse and the Chapel of Baptism and the Chapel of Penitence on either side of the Front of Glory. The portals open out into large porches, allowing the installation of iconography relating to the Birth, the Passion and the Glory. Each column is dedicated to an apostle the Catalan dioceses, the Spanish dioceses or the five continents, with the saints associated with them, in a synthesis of the universality of the Church, stretching from East to West, as the Bishop of Tarragona, Saint Fructuous prayed at the time of his martyrdom.

Present state of work on the church.

Chapel of El Carmen, with the tomb of Gaudí.

2.- The crypt

Gaudí kept to the groundplan already drawn up for the crypt, but raise the vault covering it, with a beautiful representation of the Annunciation of Mary in the keystone, so that the window would light the spot above the ambulatory surrounding it and which separates it from the chapels. He also introduced a wide moat around the crypt, keeping out the damp and letting in light. The chapels are dedicated to the members of the Holy Family of Jesus. In the centre is the Sacred Heart, flanked by the Immaculate Conception and Saint Joseph, along with Saint Joachim, Saint Anne, Saint Elizabeth and Saint Zacharias, Saint John the Baptist and Saint John the Evangelist. The Altar of Saint Joseph was inaugurated in 1885. This features neo-Gothic ornamentation Gaudí had studied in great detail.

At present, the crypt is where the life of the parish goes on. The high altar occupies the central area closest to the transept. On one side is the Holy Sacrament and on the other is the statue of Our Lady of Montserrat. A mosaic representing the vine and the grain is installed in the centre of the crypt. The chapels closing the ambulatory contain the tombs of the Bocabella and Dalmases families, as well as that of the architect, Antoni Gaudí.

Portal of the Sacristy.

Central nave of the crypt. ▷

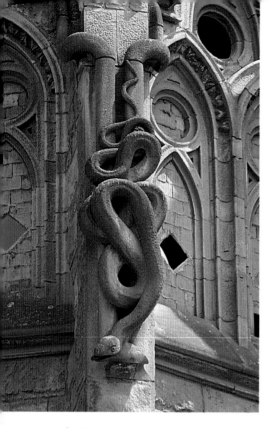

Snakes and snails in the gargoyles.

The spires terminate in plant shapes. ▷

3.- The apse

The apse, built between 1891 and 1895, is neo-Gothic in style, though it contains elements where Gaudí's personality clearly stands out. It consists of seven polygonal shaped chapels dedicated to the suffering and joy of Saint Joseph At the crown are the antiphonies of Advent, beginning with the «O».

The arrangement of the windows, the contrast of light and shade in the chapels and, especially, the gargoyles and spires of the pinnacles, take their inspiration from the flora and fauna which grew around the very building: lizards, snails and sea-snails, salamanders, frogs and tadpoles. The enlarged shoots of plants constitute an extraordinary naturalist vision at the service of architecture.

Along the separating walls of the chapels, between the carved pedestal and baldachin are the founding saints Dominic, Anthony, Benedict, Elijah, Bruno, Francis, Clare, Bernard and Teresa.

Brackets, columns and the play of light in the interior.

The Portal of the Rosary (1899). ▷

4.- The Cloister

The arrangement of the cloister, encircling the church, is very different from that of basilicas, monasteries or cathedrals. The cloister communicates portals, chapels and sacristies and, surrounding the church as it does, allows the circulation of processions whilst keeping out noise from the exterior. On the ground floor are lower spaces which can be used as workshops, services or storerooms.

Initially, Gaudí built the first two stretches on either side of the Front of the Nativity, placing portals dedicated to Our Lady of the Rosary and of Montserrat in the irregular space between the belltowers. These portals cover conical lanterns through which the daylight enters.

In order to show what could have been done, Gaudí completed the section dedicated to the Virgin of the Rosary with extraordinary craftsmanship. This is filigree work which reminds one of needlepoint or fine basket-weaving, adorned by roses and rosaries. The Virgin of the Ro-

Detail of Our Lady of the Rosary, Saint Dominic and Saint Catherine.

Decorative elements on walls, brackets and keystones. ▷

sary, with the Child, presides the archivolt of the portal, along with Saint Dominic and Saint Catherine of Sienna. On either side of the portal are the Patriarchs, kings and prophets Isaac, Jacob, David and Solomon. In the corbels of the vault groins are representations of the Death of the Righteous One and the Temptations of Man and Woman.

The text of the Ave Maria invites the faithful to make the angelic salutation, whilst the words «Et in hora mortis nostrae, Amen» give significance to the company of Jesus, Joseph and Mary as comfort to the dying. The temptations show the devil placing a bomb in the hands of a terrorist or with a purse with which he prostitutes women.

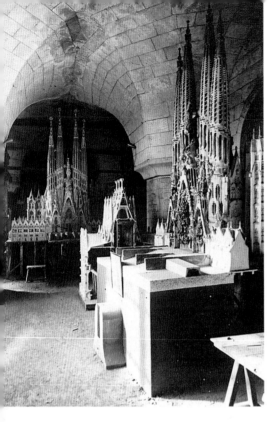

Models of the building, as they were displayed in Gaudí's time.

5.- The Nave and Aisles

The nave and aisles are made up of completely new forms with original geometric solutions and structures. Gaudí began to plan these in around 1910, incorporating his experience with the chapel of the Colonia Güell. A solution with slightly helicoidal columns, arches and vaults and with hyperbolic paraboloids was published in 1917. The discovery of the light-giving quality of hyperboloids

led to their use in the nave in a concave-convex intersection of domes coordinated with columns, walls and windows. These forms, of which 1:10 models were made, form a vision of the forest which he often used as an image to explain his project.

Gaudí considered these columns, vaults windows and roofs to be the final result desired, and a general structural presentation of this configuration was made by his assistant, the architect Sugrañes in 1923 to the Catalan Association of Architects. This 1:10 scale model as designed by Gaudí is now being turned into reality.

a) The Columns

This new form of vertical support conceived by Gaudí, leaning slightly «so as to follow the pressure curve supporting the weight of the roof» is in itself an extraordinary creative innovation.

Flutes spring from the intersection of two helicoids, beginning at the concave sections of the starred polygon and multiplying upward as they turn. The second reaches a height in metres half that of the sides of the polygon, producing twice as many new flutes. A third turn of the fourth section of the height quadruples them up to the start of the corresponding capital.

Gaudí's column is at once extraordinary and simple.

It produces flutes which become

finer and multiply as it rises, springing from the most sunken parts of each flute. As it ascends, it combines both the lightness of helicoidal growth and the gravity of the Doric column, but it is, above all, surprising, completely new and of exceptional beauty.

Restored original model of a capital, a convergence of ellipsoids.

Work inside the church.

Columns and knots (1:10 scale model).

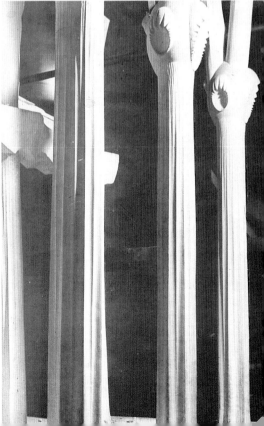

Intersections of direct or inverted hyperboloids forming the vaults.

Plaster model of the vaults, nave (1:10 scale). ▷

c) The vaults

Over the columns, the capitals are large, oval-shaped elements grouped in the upper section of the column. From them, new columns of similar generation spring like branches, leaning inwards so as the reduce the span of the vaults. The intersection of these surfaces from the tense, light whole which, as seen in the 1:10 scale model, is in itself one of the achievements –though only in plaster– which best establish Gaudí's lasting contribution to 20th century architecture.

The vaults are rich in symbols and figures, with anagrams of Jesus, Mary and Joseph on the central hyperboloids, and mosaics with angelic figures surrounding the figure of our Eternal Father at the rear of the apse, the central element in the mystical decoration Gaudí dreamt of.

c) The high windows

The length of the nave and the transept are graceful windows allowing light to filter in through geometrical forms begun in the neo-Gothic side of the Front of the Nativity, then changing into applications, though inscribed, of paraboloids, revolving and flat hyper-

Columns and lateral vaults with high windows.

boloids which, as Gaudí said, «make mouldings unnecessary, since light enters and is diffused in a play of varying intensity and colour». In the exterior, they are decorated with the fruits of each season, following they cycle of the year. These elements symbolise the fruits of the Holy Spirit which are showered on all men and women. On the mullion at the top of each window is a Founding Saint: Ignatius of Loyola, Josep de Calasanç, Joaquima de Vedruna, Antoni Maria Claret and Joan Bosco, etc.

Terminating each of these windows are baskets brimming with all kinds of fruit.

d) The roofs

These constitute one of the unique elements in the entire Sagrada Familia, despite their functional purpose –intended as they are to protect the church from the rain and other elements–. «A monumental unit of six domes lights the transept and the altar, exalting the entire church», said Gaudí, «culminating the pyramidisation of the building». Over the last few years work on the church, Gaudí had completed the

Detail of a high window in the aisle under the choir.

Lightened openwork walls of the windows in the nave.

structural study of the building of which all we know are a number of sketches showing a similar structure to that of the sacristies, though longer, with an eight-pointed star cross-section rounded off by concave paraboloids Twelve and thirteen stories divide up the great height, with small columns and a sturdy double shell. On the outside is unfaced brick and stone. The dome of Our Lady covers the apse,

Spires: original 1:10 model and completed version.

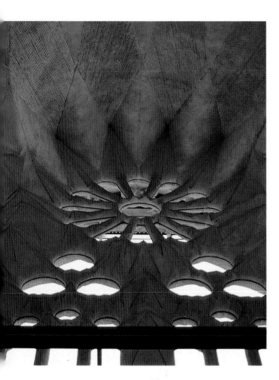

High windows in the church.

Original model of the window in the nave (1:10 scale).

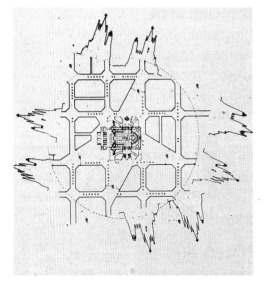

which, due to its great width, appears as a cupola.

The roof of the nave is formed by pyramids –one per section– interconnected and with large paraboloids in the front of the windows. Small structures bearing the anagrams of the Holy Family support and crown lanterns 70 metres in height, with the words «Alleluia, Amen», on parabolic shields.

Silhouette of the church as Gaudí drew it.

Original model of the nave roof. ▷

Roof of the cloister lantern.

The space between the vaults and the roof is horizontally divided into four floors which support clusters of four small inclined columns which spring from the higher ramifications of the main columns. The aisles are covered by slightly sloping surfaces featuring beautifully resolved pyramid-shaped lanterns lighting the rafters and diffusing the light.

Weather-resistant stone from Montjuïc was proposed for the outer layer of the roof. With structural supports –floors and small columns, and the vaults making up the interior view– Gaudí's basic premise is ever-present: «Divide the inert loads and multiply the active elements».

Restored model of the nave and aisles, façades and roofs of the Nativity and the Passion.

Night-time view of the church.

Nativity Façade (June 1997).

6.- The façades

Each of these has three portals symbolising the theological virtues of Faith, Hope and Charity and are crowned by four belltowers representing the Apostles. On these can be read the words «Sanctus, Hosanna Excelsis», for Gaudí wanted all, on reading this inscription, to praise the Lord.

a) Nativity Façade:
In the central archivolt, under the Star of the Orient, are Jesus, Mary and Joseph, between the ox and the mule, surrounded by singing angels. On either side are the Adoration of the Shepherds and the Magi. Higher up angels play trumpets announcing the Nativity, the Annunciation and the Coronation of Mary. Finally, there is a cypress tree, the refuge of birds, symbolising the Church as a huge spire crowned by a «Tau», the Greek initial letter designating the name of God. On the south side, around the Door of Hope, is the Wedding of Joseph and Mary, the Flight to Egypt, the Massacre of the Innocents, the nave of the Church steered by Joseph and, on the spire, the rock of Montserrat inscribed with the word «Sálvanos»

(«Save us»). On the other side is the Door of Faith, represented by the Visitation, Christ amongst the Doctors, the Presentation in the Temple and Jesus the Worker in his carpentry shop. In the spires are ears of wheat and grapes with the image of Mary in the dogma of the Immaculate.

b) Façade of the Passion:
Desolation, pain, sacrifice and death provide the counterpoint in the west front, which is presided over by the death of Christ so that his Resurrection and Ascension into Heaven can be proclaimed from the heights. The portal was planned in pain, after 1911, when Gaudí, ill in Puigcerdà had time on his hands to study and meditate on it. «I am ready», he said, «to sacrifice the building itself, to smash vaults and cut columns in order to give an idea of the cruelty of sacrifice».

The sculptor Josep Maria Subirachs created around 100 figures evoking the Passion of Christ, beginning with the figure of Christ on the Column in the mullion of the central portal.

Alone, the figure of Jesus bound is flanked on either side by the Betrayal of Judas and the Denial of Peter.

Portal of Hope: The Flight to Egypt, The Massacre of the Innocents and Joseph with the Child.

Portal of Faith: Jesus among the Doctors and Jesus at Work.

The Holy Family under the Star of Kings.

The spires of the Nativity Façade. ▷

Veronica: Vía Dolorosa.
The Last Supper.
The Denial of Peter.
Ecce Homo.
Sculptures by Josep Maria Subirachs.

Composition of stars, seen from a balcony.

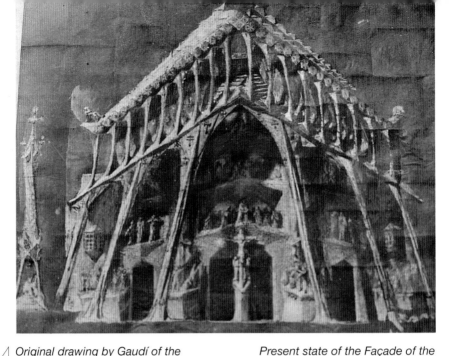

Present state of the Façade of the Passion.

Above, the *Via Dolorosa,* with Jesus carrying the Cross after being condemned by Pilate. The figure of Veronica is at the centre, showing the image of the «Man of Pain», a face seen in negative, enveloped in mystery. Mary, Saint John, the Holy Women, the soldiers, the people... figures leading up to the scene of the Holy Sepulchre.

The image of Christ Resurrected ascending to Heaven, between the belltowers, will complete the representation of the human life of Christ in the catechistic vision of the Mystery of our Salvation.

c) Façade of the Glory:
Gaudí left a study of the volumes and structure and of the iconographic and symbolic design of this main façade, which faces towards the sea. A monumental narthex gives way to three portals and is crowned by four belltowers flanked on either side by the Chapel of the Sacrament and the Baptistery.

There are eleven doors leading directly or through the cloister into the chapels, and from these into the church itself. The central portal has three doors. The narthex is covered by the vaults under the belltower, hyperboloids and 15 lanterns. These are asymmetrical hyperboloids which cut and crown various cones. All is supported in view, on 21 columns, except for the connecting walls between the chapels and under the belltowers. The whole forms a large tympanum with ascending hyperboloids in which Gaudí envi-

Jesus on the column (J. M. Subirachs).

sioned an iconographic representation of the Glory.

Stony clouds are inscribed with the symbol of Faith, the Credo. The entrance, at the same level as the entire church, is high enough above Carrer Mallorca for this route to continue circulating below, and thus the narthex opens out into a great open space. On either side Gaudí imagined a 20 metre high waterspout and a huge flaming cresset purifying fire and water. The iconography presents man within the Order of Creation, his origin and his end, with the Way to achieve it. «Since Adam and Eve, through hard work and by practicing virtue, man can conquer the Glory Christ opened for us through Redemption and with the help of Grace». We also find here the Beatitudes, the Virtues and the capital sins: Hell is represented beneath the vaults of the street. Higher up is Purgatory and, over each of the seven entrance doors, representing the Sacraments, is a prayer to Our Father.

In the centre of the façade is Saint Joseph at work, with the attributes of the manual trades. Higher up, Mary presides as a Queen over the Saints, whilst at the top is Christ with the attributes of the Passion, with the seven trumpeting angels announcing the Last Judgement. The angel hierarchies surround the Eternal Father and, in the large central rose window, the Holy Spirit completes this vision of the Trinity.

Original model of the study of volumes for the Façade of the Glory.

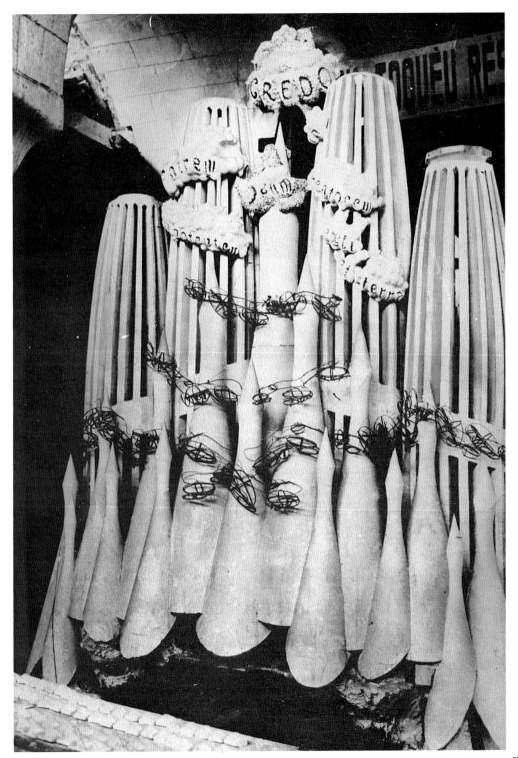

7. Sacristies and chapels

«The paraboloid is the father of all geometry», Gaudí said. Featuring an outstanding composition of these planes, he projected the double-faced cupola-like structures situated in the north and west corners of the cloister, leaving the angles covered by lanterns dedicated to the Ember days of Autumn and to the Advent. The cupola arris and the large parabolic spherical lunes of the extrados, of bare brick, are graceful and will be decorated with mosaics.

The Baptistery and the Chapel of the Sacrament occupy the corners of the main front. A rough sketch by Gaudí shows a structure supported by central columns and the enveloping penetration of the cloister.

Externally similar to the sacristies, their corners also contain small chapels and lanterns dedicated to the Ember days of Lent and Pentecost.

1:25 scale model of the Sacristy.

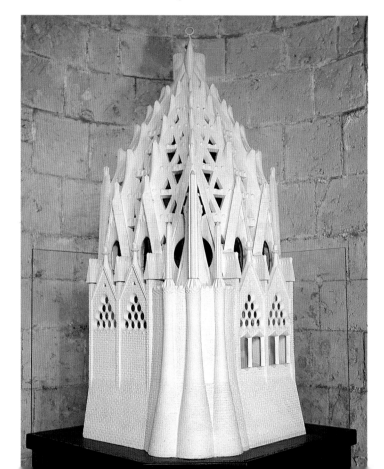

The church seen from the east. Study carried out under the direction of Puig Boada and Bonet Garí.

ept and apse are crowned with a further six domes dedicated to Jesus Christ, the Four Evangelists and Our Lady. The highest of these will be culminated by a 170 metre high cross. During the day, this will sparkle with mosaics, at night with spotlights which will be installed on it to illuminate the other belltowers and, from them, the whole city in enactment of the words of Jesus, «I am the light» (John, 8, 12).

Gaudí worked long on the termination of the belltowers. In the model presented at the Paris Exhibition in 1910, the solution he planned was

Present state of the works.

8.- The Belltowers and Domes

The first Belltower of Saint Barnabas first came into view on 30 November 1925. Gaudí expressed his delight at seeing how «That lance joined the heavens with the earth». The other three were completed by the architect Sugrañes, the master's successor and collaborator, who left the Nativity Façade almost complete. Twelve belltowers are included in the plans, reaching a height of from 98 to 112 metres over the floor of the church. In the Nativity Façade are Matthew, Judas, Simon and Barnabas, in that of the Passion, James, Bartholomew, Thomas and Philip, and in the Façade of the Glory are Andrew, Peter, Paul and James. The trans-

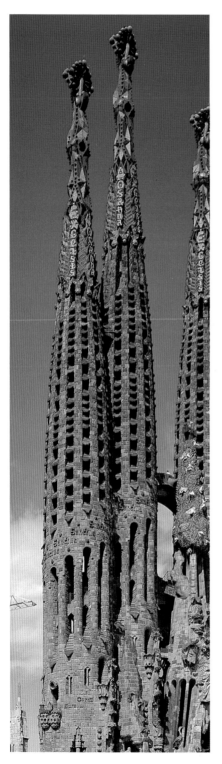

Belltower of Saint Barnabas.

quite different: so-called «pineapple beacons» were to receive and project rays of symbolic light. Lack of resources, however, gave Gaudí more time to compose the geometrical figures symbolising the Apostles with the episcopal attributes, the ring, the mitre, the crosier and the cross. The almost 25 metre high terminations begin with letters proclaiming «Hosanna Excelsis» in an enveloping hexagonal ascending order, separating channels formed by dihedral angles decorated with pyramid-shaped encircling dark-green glazed baked brick.

Next, starred geometrical forms of gold and silver Venetian mosaics on a red background rise to converge at the confluence of the octahedron and a perforated sphere housing the reflectors and representing the episcopal ring. A triangular pyramid-shaped trunk curves round, forming the crosier, whilst two diverging curvilinear squares reveal the mitre as they mark out the cross.

The belltowers emerge from the mass of the three great portals in each façade, dedicated to the theological virtue. They have a double gallery in which ascend in the interior a helicoidal staircase, rising between the chiaroscuro of the ribs of vertical stone and the inclined planes ascending vertically. The interior space will be installed with tubular bells, designed by Gaudí to ring out all around.

Interior of a belltower. ▷

Detail of a boss from a mosaic.

Starred decorative element with a
Venetian mosaic.

The episcopal symbols: the cross, the
ring, the mitre and the crosier. ▷

Sketch made by Le Corbusier during his visit.

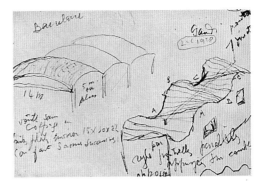

Roofs of the schools.

9.- The Schools

The parish schools were built in 1909 so as to begin implementing the provisional programme of the church. For this reason, the partly sunken floor of the aisles and a section of the cloisters is set aside for these schools. As Gaudí said: «by the side of the Church, the people will receive education and culture». The construction of a low-cost building adequate to fulfil this purpose was therefore undertaken on the large site available. In it, Gaudí demonstrated his enormous architectural capacity with surprising simplicity and complexity. Inside, inclined vertical partition walls support beams supporting and undulating roof, going from concave to convex in order to collect water and, at the same time, give greater structural resistance. The roofed span over the three classrooms was divided in half so that planks of standard length and section could be used. Standing wooden beams and a cross-beam running the length of the building divide the rectangle around the perimeter.

A fire started by revolutionary extremists in July 1936 destroyed the schools, which were later rebuilt by the architect Quintana with a number of modifications to the original plans.

Period photograph of a class.

◁ *The Church Schools.*

Model made to calculate and project the Chapel of the Colonia Güell.

THE STRUCTURE

Gaudí drew up his first plans for the church in Gothic style. He stressed the verticality of the elements, however, as can be appreciated in his sketch of the entire building seen from the apse («El Propagador», 1891).

The extraordinary and intelligent solution of raising the Nativity Façade thanks to the possibilities afforded by the reception of a large donation led to the prolongation of the study carried out to draw up the overall plan for the church. The economic precariousness of the project was, in fact, a help, contributing to the fact that Gaudí devoted the last twelve years of his life to clearing the way to making the Sagrada Familia the most important architectural feat of the 20th century, structurally speaking.

In the search for pressure curves and the desire for the forms to coincide, he decided to incline the columns, identifying the mechanical and architectural organism in each element. The result was an arboreal, balanced, light structure which would have made it possible, had it been built 70 years ago, to considerably reduce the scaffolding necessary for any Gothic cathedral. Moreover, Gaudí selected the most resistant natural materials capable of supporting the heavy loads supported by the other domes and stone roofs planned which, at the same time, fireproofed the building, their loads also helping to absorb seismic tremors.

Now, using computers, the feasibility of Gaudí's original project has been fully demonstrated.

SYMBOLISM

«The entire Church of the Sagrada Familia is a hymn of praise to God intoned by Humanity and of which each stone is a verse sung in a clear, powerful, harmonious voice», writes Puig Boada. It was clear to Gaudí that this was to be the church of the people, a song to the Trinity of God. In its exterior, the Sagrada Familia building symbolises the Church, Jesus Christ and the faithful, represented by Mary, the Apostles and the Saints. The twelve belltowers represent the Apostles, the first bishops of the Church, the voice which exhorts the faithful, enlarged witnesses to the revelation received.

Inside, the columns supporting the vaults and roof also represent the Apostles and the local churches with their saints, that is to say, everyone, from the Catalan dioceses to those of the five continents, as well as celestial Jerusalem, the mystical city

Wrought-iron sword traversing Mary, Alpha and Omega.

of peace the Lamb of God has won for us.

Gaudí said that the nave and aisles and the vaults would be «Like a forest. Light will enter in abundance through windows placed at different heights. It will be possible to follow the main daily prayers (the Te Deum, the Miserere, the Benedictus and the Magnificat) from the inscriptions on the handrails of the choir and the triforiums». Outstanding of the columns encircling the transept and apse, dedicated to the Apostles and the Evangelists, are those of the Apostles Peter and Paul, which join the triumphal arch with the Calvary, the Virgin Mary, the Crucifixion and Saint John. The representation of the Trinity will be completed by the image of the Eternal Father which will be seen by entering the church in the dome of the apse with a seven-armed lamp, symbolising the Holy Spirit. The inscription of the Hymn of Glory and the hanging canopy which protects the altar, will centre the attention of worshippers here. In the triforium on the side of the Façade of the Passion is the Virgin Mary, surrounded by angels with the attributes of the Litanies. In that of the Nativity is Saint Joseph with the attributes of his trade, completing, along with the crucifix at the altar, the representation of the Holy Family.

Signs of the zodiac in the pointed arch of the Annunciation.

The Portal of Charity in the Nativity Façade.

47

Detail of the interior of the Nativity Façade.

PLASTICITY

For any work of architecture to be considered beautiful, its elements must have be appropriately located and be fitting in size, shape and colour.

a) Nature.
Gaudí's plasticity is based on his study of nature, and is expressed in forms and colours. As mentioned previously, Gaudí commented on his learning from nature as follows: «This tree, next to my workshop, is my master». Observing it, he drew conclusions which he put into practice in his projects. The use of natural forms, of flora and fauna, is frequent throughout his work and in many of the details of the Church of the Sagrada Familia. Abstract geometrical forms are derived from the study of nature, the result od combinations od convereences and new forms which had never before been used in architecture.

Sculpture representing the Flight to Egypt.

Turtle forming the base of a column in the Portal of the Nativity.

The snail and the lizard represent the local fauna.

Spiral staircase imitating natural forms. ▷

Christmas weather is evoked by the large icicles adorning the three portals of the Nativity.

Wrought-iron torch-stand.

Arched gallery in the interior of the Nativity Façade.

b) Form.

Natural forms are present even in the capitals in the crypt and the gargoyles and spires of the apse. In the Nativity Façade, the human figure, plants and animals are present, expressing the Mystery of the Nativity, with all that which surrounds the childhood of Jesus. They are also found in the windows, in the sculptural motifs representing fruits from the different seasons of the year. Geometrical forms based on simple elements and drawings became more complicated as the study and use of curved surfaces became more familiar to Gaudí. He first made use of paraboloids, then hyperboloids, producing a great range of theoretic and formal innovation. The columns, windows and vaults Gaudí planned in the later years of his life are the exponent of an extraordinary work of research and study. This is also true of the belltowers, the domes and other elements.

Detail of the Portal of the Rosary. ▷

Detail of the wrought-iron fence.

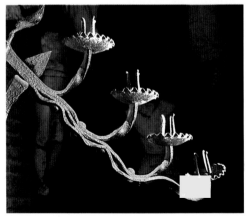

Wrought-iron candelabrum.

Moveable pulpit.

Geometric compositions in the nave vaults. ▷

Elements of trencadis mosaic on a provisional construction.

c) Colour.

Colour is another important element in Gaudí's architecture. In the Church of the Sagrada Familia, the terminations of the belltowers are the finest exponent of the results obtained from his use of colour. A model demonstrating Gaudí's ideas for the Nativity Façade in a scale of 1:25 was made for the Paris Exhibition in 1910, but was, unfortunately, destroyed in 1936. From it however, Gaudí's theories were applied in the chapel in the Colonia Güell and other works.

Coloured model made in 1910.

Stained-glass windows in the crypt.

Terminals of the belltowers.

d) Acoustics and lighting.

Gaudí had studied acoustic problems and experimented with the tubular bells he installed in the elongated hollowed sections of the belltowers, as well as with the organs which were to fill the nave and aisles with resounding music. There are singers' galleries surrounding the nave, in the interior of the rear section of the Façade of the Glory, with capacity for 1,500 singers, and over the ambulatory in the apse, where there is space for a choir of 700 children. With the priests surrounding the altar, Gaudí felt certain that the people would take part in services, in this ahead of the II Vatican Council, as he was in many other decisions of a liturgical nature. Light, harmoniously entering through the large high windows, diffused by the new geometrical surfaces, will prevent excessive contrasts, giving greater visibility to the decorated surfaces. Spotlights placed at the mouths of the hyperboloids of the vaults add diffused lighting at night, accompanied by that from the stained glass windows, leaded in accordance with the new procedure tried out in Majorca Cathedral with maximum brilliance of the polychrome glass, without paint or enamelwork. «The church will be full of light, with beautiful variations, combining that coming in from the domes with that from the glass of the high windows. All this will illuminate the polychrome of the interior», as Gaudí explained.

Hollow of the belltowers for reflectors.

Soundwings to project music and singing.

d) Liturgical objects.

Gaudí planned the altars, objects and furnishings for worship in the church, giving us liturgical instruction through the dignity and quality of each item: the benches, the sacristy cupboards, the pulpit and the confessional boxes, the candelabras and the credence tables, the seats for the officiants, the lamps and the chandeliers. Particularly outstanding are the candlestand and the lectern. Gaudí himself had a personal hand in making some of these pieces.

Holy Week candle.

Candelabrum for Holy Week.
Cross with candelabrum.

Joan Maragall (drawing by R. Casas), promoter of the Church of the Sagrada Familia.

PRESENT STATE AND IMMEDIATE FUTURE

Today, only half of the building can be considered complete. The finished elements are the crypt, the walls enclosing the apse, the Nativity and Passion façades (the pediment and high window have still to be completed in this front) with their bell-towers; the fronts of the aisles and the crossing with vaults 30 m² in height and covering an area of 1,000 m². The high windows in the nave are being built and the vaults begun, along with the singers' galleries in the nave and part of the nave vaults.

The faithful and friends of the Church of the Sagrada Familia are the spiritual support behind this idea, keeping it moving forward, and work continues thanks to the donations, large and small, which are received daily. To this must be added the selfless dedication of all those working on the project: technicians, masons, sculptors, stone-cutters, mechanics, carpenters, etc.

The administration is austere, making it possible to adjust work to the rhythm of income is received in the form of donations of all types. This is an expiatory church and can, therefore, be built only using alms.

Technically, the most modern technology is employed: computers to calculate the structure or work the stone, together with quality control of the stone and concrete used, or the machinery for shoring up the foundations.

Everybody asks, «When will it be finished?» This is a difficult question to answer, as it is condition by the donations received, but there is a programme for the present and the immediate future which is successfully putting into practice the proposals put forward by the Foundation's Board of Trustees.

Gaudí took from 40 to 50 years to build just one façade along with the crypt and the walls of the apse. Then came the upheaval of the Spanish Civil War, which saw the work paralysed for some 20 years. The generation of those who knew Gaudí –his direct followers– took another 20 years to complete the Façade of the Passion. The challenge now is to terminate the vaults by the beginning of the 21st century, but even then there will still be much to do: the domes of the crossing and apse have to be raised, the roofs and the Façade of the Glory built, and all those elements Gaudí left in the form of precise ideas, like a dream of the future, made reality.

LOVERS OF THE CHURCH OF THE SAGRADA FAMILIA

«The Church of the Sagrada Familia is being built by the people and is a reflection of their way of being. In the Sagrada Familia, everything is providential», Gaudí used often to repeat, adding that this would be «the church of present-day Catalonia». The poet Joan Maragall, a great friend of Gaudí, was the first to realise the transcendence of the master's work, and was his first sponsor in the press.

A series of circumstances conspired to wipe the church from the face of the earth: the schools were destroyed, Gaudí's studio disappeared, though not his spirit. Interest began once more to be kindled after the centenary of the architect's death in 1952. Until then, no art history book mentioned him, not famous historian had heard of him. With the controversy over whether the work should continue or not, the arguments which began with the silence which had surrounded the last years of Gaudí's life also began to be aired once more. But the people continued faithful to him, and

President Prat de la Riba and Bishop Reig listen to Gaudí's explanations.

alms and donations arrived. The collection, announced one Sunday each year, receives ever-greater support. «This work is in the hands of God and the will of the people», Gaudí would say. The Catalans have responded generously and have fallen in love with the growing church, «their» church. And, as Gaudí said, prophetically, «People from all over the world will come to admire it». The image of the Church of the Sagrada Familia has come to symbolise the whole city of Barcelona. Shortly after the death of Gaudí, a

Mn. Rangonesi, listening to Gaudí, exclaimed «You are the Dante of architecture!».

Torres i Bages and Gaudí. Drawing by Opisso.

young Japanese architect, Kenji Imai, arrived in Barcelona. He did not meet the master, but was so deeply impressed by his work that he made it widely known in Japan. He even dared build the cathedral in Nagasaki following the ideas his study of Gaudí's work had inspired in him. Since then, Japanese people come to see his works because they know him to be one of the great masters of modern architecture. In the 1950s, the German architect Gropius visited the Chapel of the Colonia Güell, staying there for over an hour in silent contemplation of that marvel. Le Corbusier reproduced the church schools in a sketch in 1927 after his first visit to Barcelona, later writing about Gaudí that he is «this century's great builder». In Paris in 1961 the exhibition on «The Origins of the 20th Century» won recognition for the achievement of Gaudí, which had not be understood in 1910. In Italy, in Britain, in Holland, in Germany or in New Zealand, all over the world, Gaudí's originality is finally acclaimed and the architect is considered one of the greatest exponents in the entire history of art. His Holiness Pope John Paul II took in the Sagrada Familia as part of his visit to Barcelona and, indeed, no visiting figure from the world of politics, art or science fails to visit this renowned monument. To visit a church under construction. An unusual experience.

Pope John Paul II on his visit to the Sagrada Familia in 1982.

Chronology of the Church of the Sagrada Familia:

1886   Josep Maria Bocabella founds the «Associació de Devots de Sant Josep» (Association of Followers of Saint Joseph), which would become the promoter of the Church of the Sagrada Familia.

1882   First stone laid. Project by architect Villar.

1883   Antoni Gaudí becomes the architect of the church.

1889   The crypt is finished.

1890   Drawing of the first overall solution.

1892   Work begins on Nativity Façade.

1894   Apse front completed.

1899   Completion of the Portal of the Rosary in the cloister.

1909   Building of the parish school.

1910   Exhibition in Paris of the model of the Nativity Façade.

1917   Project for the Façade of the Passion, with the monument to Bishop Torres i Bages.

1923   Final solution for nave, aisles and roofs in 1:10 and 1:25 scale plaster models.

1925   30 November. First belltower (Saint Barnabas), 100 metres high, finished.

1926   Antoni Gaudí dies in an accident on 10 June.

1930   The four belltowers of the Nativity Façade completed.

1936   Spanish Civil War. Profanation and destruction in the church. Gaudí's studio destroyed.

1940   Restoration of the crypt and plaster models.

1954   Work begins on the Façade of the Passion.

1977   The four belltowers of the Façade of the Passion completed.

1978   Work begins on the fronts of the nave and aisles.

1986-90 Foundations of the nave and aisles. First sculptures for the Façade of the Passion.

1995   Construction of the aisle vaults.

1997   Construction of the nave.

Antoni Gaudí at the Corpus Christi procession in 1924, on the steps of Barcelona Cathedral.

EPILOGUE

Whether or not the work of building the Temple Expiatori de la Sagrada Família continues depends, fundamentally, on the public will. A few years ago, before the nave and aisles began to be built, Cardinal Jubany, Archbishop of Barcelona, took the decision that it should be so because the will of the people was being expressed in the constant contribution of donations, mostly small amounts, but many in number, accompanied from time to time by larger gifts or legacies.

Why do people ask insistently the question «When will the Sagrada Familia be finished?» Gaudí himself was asked this question, and he replied «My client is in no hurry». Why does the monument receive so many visitors? It is difficult to answer this question, but the construction of this church, dedicated to Jesus, Mary and Joseph, the Holy Family of Nazareth, is the expression of solidarity, of Faith and Hope embraced by Love which, with its invocation of God the Father, our Creator, is the sign of the brotherhood of all human beings.

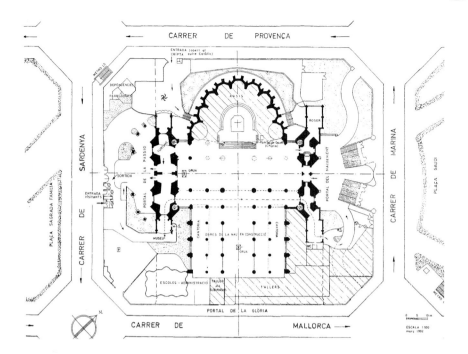

THE VISIT

Today, starting from the entrance in Plaça de la Sagrada Família, one can visit:

– The Façade of the Passion, work on which continues. A lift takes visitors to a height of 90 metres.

– The interior of what will be the cathedral, between the eight points of the east and west front belltowers.

– The apse and its walls with their long windows, the crossing columns and the nave.

– The aisles and their vaults and singers' galleries, along with part of the vaults in the nave.

– The whole of the Nativity Façade, where a lift takes visitors up to a height of 60 metres.

– The monographic museum, showing the history of the church and many of Antoni Gaudí's original plaster models, liturgical objects, photos, plans, etc. A special exhibition room contains some twenty original drawings by Gaudí.

– In the crypt, open for the services of the parish church, are the tombs of Gaudí and the founders of the building.

– The map shows the location of the main elements, giving information which can be complemented at the administrative offices of the Temple Expiatori de la Sagrada Família.

EDITORIAL ESCUDO DE ORO, S.A.
I.S.B.N. 84-378-1923-7
Printed by FISA - Escudo de Oro, S.A.
Palaudarias, 26 - 08004 Barcelona
Dep. Legal B. 34018-1997